The Battle of
Heptonstall

The Battle of Heptonstall

Michael Crowley

Smoke Stack Books

Smokestack Books
1 Lake Terrace, Grewelthorpe, Ripon HG4 3BU
e-mail: info@smokestack-books.co.uk
www.smokestack-books.co.uk

Copyright 2021,
Michael Crowley

ISBN 9781838198824

Smokestack Books
is represented
by Inpress Ltd

I think that the poorest he that is in England hath a life to live as the greatest he; every man that is to live under a government ought first by his own consent to put himself under that government.

Leveller MP
Thomas Rainsborough,
Putney debates 1647

*for Rosa
and Charlie*

A poem is an afterlife on earth.

Les Murray

Contents

Introduction	10

The Battle of Heptonstall

Weaver	15
Spinner	16
Nothing but Labour	17
Spinster	18
Wool Master	19
Promise	20
Pike-Man	21
Seeker	22
Reason	23
Unreason	24
The Orphan Rose	25
Heresy	26
Babylon	27
Execution of a Ghost	28
Rosehips	29
Lodger	30
Billet	31
Cockcroft's Soldier	32
Spy	33
Wind of Doubt	34
Sinful	36
Pilgrim	37
Murder and Remorse	38
Fretful	39
Night March	40
Fight or Flee	41
Victory	42
Apology	43
God's Work	44
Forsaken	45
Did I Plant Anew?	46
Ballad of the Battle of Heptonstall	47
Visitor	49

Aftermath
- Cursed — 53
- Sealed Knot — 54
- Squaddie — 55
- Veterans in Recovery — 56
- Soldier's Boy — 57
- Chances Are — 58
- The Hand That Crossed the Paper — 60
- Arboriculture — 61
- Fire-Bug — 62
- Break-in at the Gallery of Justice — 63
- Hold That Thought — 64
- The Village — 65
- Gone — 66
- Heptonstall Garden in June — 67
- Low Pressure — 68
- Pub Landlord West Yorkshire — 69
- Dogs Own Country — 71
- St Thomas the Apostle Church, Heptonstall — 72
- Keighley Railway Museum — 73
- The Day-Trip — 74
- Plagued — 75
- Incurable — 76
- Aftermath — 77
- Last Day of the Shrine — 78
- Back and Forth — 79

Acknowledgements — 80

Introduction

The Battle of Heptonstall took place in November 1643 during the early part of the English Civil War. Some argue it was more of a skirmish than a battle because the dead would have been counted in scores or in the low hundreds and when one thinks of Civil War battles, we tend to think of the large-scale set pieces such as Naseby, where the number killed was at least a thousand. But what happened at Heptonstall was more typical and a more regular feature of a conflict that lasted almost ten years across Britain and Ireland. A series of wars that in England left behind a death toll higher per head of the population than the First World War, and in Ireland proportionally greater even than the famine of the mid nineteenth century.

Heptonstall is a hilltop village in the West Riding and at the time much of its population was employed in the wool trade. In the West Riding the majority supported parliament's cause against the king, but in 1643 the region was under military control of royalist armies that pillaged for food, money, arms and recruits. In response Colonel Robert Bradshaw led eight hundred and fifty parliamentary troops from Lancashire to Heptonstall almost outnumbering the inhabitants. A few weeks later, Sir Francis Mackworth marched eight hundred royalist cavalry and foot soldiers the seven miles from Halifax, through the night of 1st November, in an attempt to seize the village. The terrain was difficult, rain had swollen the river below whilst Bradshaw's men, who were forewarned of the attack, crashed boulders and musket balls down on the royalists as they tried to climb the hill. They were driven back and many drowned in their attempts to escape. Parliament's victory was short lived for in January of 1644, Mackworth returned with greater numbers, forcing the parliamentarians to retreat west into Lancashire. The royalists sacked Heptonstall burning barns and houses and taking all the livestock. The village paid a heavy price for being caught between two sides. More widely the war destroyed the wool trade for some time, brought plague and the sacking of churches in a final throw of the Reformation.

The first sequence of this collection grew out of a community play I wrote for the 375th anniversary of the battle produced in the following spring of 2019. The poems enter the historical narrative through the door of a family of clothiers in the weeks leading up to the battle. The majority of the characters are imaginary though Bradshaw, Mackworth and the parish priest of the day Gilbodie, get their say. The play was funded by Sky Arts through a Brexit and the arts related initiative because of the supposed parallels between contemporary divisions in the UK and the great schism of the 1640's. It is strange how some themes remain unresolved four hundred years later, how questions refuse to lie down but then this is Britain and history isn't in the past. Such echoes make their way into the second sequence. Poetry might be an unusual and unsatisfactory way to respond to issues of government and consent, of religiously driven violence, but it is necessary and currently preferable to other courses of action.

Michael Crowley
Heptonstall,
May 2019

The Battle of Heptonstall

Weaver

John Cockcroft

All else depends on warp and weft,
that the tension be right and be even,
or the coat unravels from the back.

I make a cloth of simple tabby weave
the shafts and shuttle like it well,
all day tying to the heddles until my eyes fail.

Soldiers on the hills: the arc of their helmets,
rumps of their horses, cloth torn by blade and shot.
The summer shearing, weaving under the moon,
those days passed for another year.

Spinner

Alice Cockcroft

Thread bleeds from my palm
spindle hungry as a lamb,
wheel she turns with just a stroke
walking me closer to autumn.

I watched mother through its spokes
straw between my toes,
she laid my hands upon the fleece
I stand where she stood years ago.

I wear her smock ripe with rosemary
singing, *Although I am a country lass
a lusty mind I bear-a*, the wheel is turning
turning a lullaby back to me.

Nothing but Labour

Joseph Cockcroft

We are all at the wool each day.
Mother walks to her wheel and then away
like the hare-brained not knowing her mind.
Father he is in the loft weaving thread upon thread
even at candle light. Crow's feet for fingers,
crooked when he stands, his eyes weakening
and I, kneeling upon the stone
carding grey strands, softer than his beard
when he could lift me with his hands.

All the summer days are such.
Other lads and lasses are about from May
but not a clothier's son, I only see
wild roses on a Sunday.
My brother gone to clerk in Leeds
no one left but me to weave.
Father curses the merchants at the cloth hall
thumbing each piece, playing doubtful.
When the cloth is sold, he only buys more wool.

Spinster

Two wheels for the three of us is enough,
we have our livestock and a kitchen garden to pluck.
Hope, she shears and clod-moulds the earth,
Rose, she spins and sings. They are sistren now.

Alice comes to us for mutton,
they have no earth of their own the clothiers.
She will join our circle of prayer soon I'm certain,
hiding from the Spirit for now.

Today I opened the book at Matthew,
did find the words I already knew.
My finger leads my lips, tears bleed for the meek,
I speak to the multitude from the mountain.

Wool Master

I hear the scratching of fleeces behind doors,
the clapping of the loom from the lofts,
I smell the pots stirring.

They are rough about the price
saying the sheep has died of sickness,
believing they see the livestock with their hands.

They say for themselves what the Bible does say,
observe their own Saints days at the tavern,
do not remove their hats in church.

I walk these wet hills for them.
Lambs quiver 'neath the sodden sheep,
eyes half closed against the walls.

Soldiers' horses swim through the mist,
the cloth hall drains – the end of a heady evening.
The weavers' shoddy patience is wearing thin.

Promise

Rose

I am a girl orphaned by the plague.
Too young yet to be wed I did walk down
one hill up another making my way
inside a storm, was found by Martha
hungered, near dead. She did warm me
and feed me, swathe me in a shawl, this man
William called. *Blessed are those that mourn*
he said. His words hide within these walls.

Sweet lipped, so gentle tongued he, his eyes
see through the years to my children,
he can hear what isn't yet spoken. We the despised
are not for church, the statues and the kneeling.
Princes will fall, the world shall be made anew.
I card the fleece, bathe his feet, brush his pilgrim shoes.

Pike-man

*Sergeant Richard Leach at the Battle of Adwalton Moor,
June 1643*

We splay out as wolves to keep the horses at bay.
The first charge a taunt veering away
before they reach our points.

I have sawn two feet from my stave
an arm beyond my arms,
a quill pushed into the dough of horses and men.

The riders are knee to knee,
the mounts neck to neck
thudding louder, mud thrown higher,

swords drawn later. The beasts know
it will be blood. We are bent low,
a rocking head brings me its eyes like eggs.

My pike trembles in its acorn breast,
blood bursts back at me, soaks my head,
the beast screams, falls like an oak.

The gentleman rider I slay
his last look bearing no blame,
his last breath warming my blade.

The horse gallops the air dancing a spasm,
its eyes have knowledge of the end
but not of the victory won.

I run and lie in the womb of a clough,
quiver til nightfall. They will not charge
so easily up the hill to Heptonstall.

Seeker

William Saltmarsh, evangelist preacher, 16 October 1643

The clergy lead the people like horses,
ride them at their pleasure. They are holy
imbeciles who believe imagery forces
people to Christ. Spirit is all. It knows
all things, was before sin's invention,
the preaching of perfection. I saw a man
standing inside a tree, he clapped his hands
upon his breast saying "heaven is within me,

within me." We meet at the foot of the rocks
under the blackthorn crest, we hold hands
in the silences, the scuffle of frogs,
a warning from a jackdaw. My child Evelyn scans
the skyline for glove puppets of cavalry.
Tongues are bored, ears sawn off in the pillory.

Reason

Colonel Robert Bradshaw, Rochdale, 18 October

What does it mean to fight a king, treason?
A king that hath sent his parliament away
like a lord discharging his servants, believing
saints will cook his supper for him. He lays
with a papist plotting, with rebels turning
church into a place of coloured dolls, painted
walls and altar rails, where men kneeling
upon their own minds recite some scroll

by the Archbishop Laud. Kings are not God.
We do not seek to slay him, make him a ghost
behind palace walls, but we shall sit at his table
beside a fire of the relics and the yoke.
High birth and unearned wealth shall fall.
We make our stand hereafter at Heptonstall.

Unreason

Sir Francis Mackworth, Halifax, 20 October

A whole people think popery at their doors.
Scandalous pamphlets pour oil on the flames
demanding liberty of conscience so called,
of men's houses and men's wives. They do defame
his majesty, but those who speak of the
King's part they are marked down to be killed.
The times are a distemper where men's hearts
beat as drums mustering a blood-filled fury.

People will think it strange there were such days
when brother killed brother, when friend wished
death upon friend. God has given man unto a craze,
reason is drowned and gone mute as the fishes.
Upon a hilltop there are roundheads aplenty.
They are in need of Christ and nightly await my cavalry.

The Orphan Rose

Joseph Cockcroft on meeting Rose

Their house hides down a nook 'neath the moor.
The grass it is deep, the ditches too,
she lay crying in one when she was found,
a lamb without its ewe.

Wool master says the spinsters are witches,
this I do not know.
They live beyond the commands of men,
the old woman Martha, her sister Hope, the orphan Rose.

She wears half skirts and will not curtsey,
strumpet dressed mother says.
Her face a potion, her voice like ale,
a voyage my nights, a torment my days.

A preacher comes to stay each week,
Rose rehearses his words to the world
speaking ill of priests and princes,
words that do not belong to an orphan girl.

Heresy

Squire Thornfield, representative of Sir William Saville

Parliament worships trade, exalts treason,
heresy the liturgy, soldiering its creed
observed by clothiers huddling in caves
spinning hair, ferreting each farthing,
each day's scurry the same as the last.
They do not toil under heavenly skies,
their eyes famished of God's firmament.
Ploughing earth at the mercy of the sun
reminds man of his position: a worm
upon the ground. They are peacock proud,
forgetting all fealty but to money that grows
upon a waddling back.
                        The roots of the levelling:
leaving children without sacrament
so they might scratch an animal's back,
feed their souls into a spinning wheel.

Babylon

Father Robert Gilbodie, Heptonstall, 23 October

This day a man brandished a catechism
he held it in the air like a sword
saying we should abhor all superstition
tear down the crosses, burn the book of prayer.

Parliament's men broke my font with hammers
elsewhere they baptised their horses with urine,
their fathers having lime-washed the walls
damming unlettered men to blindness. I shall remain

but not as a martyr. I think this nation
shall become slavish and cruel to all it touches,
a callus on the palms of Christendom.
The vicarage is cold, the candle light crouches.
Of wood once left at my door, I have none.
Their campfires burn, I walk the streets alone.

Execution of a Ghost

Edmund Reeve on his father's execution in 1606

I am a man of fealty
of the old religion
from an old family
come from the corners of the north.

I did not see your execution,
when I was older though
in a doublet and breeches,
a toothless man hoisted me to a cart

to watch the bloody theatre
where a man behind a mask
pretended another is a beast,
lifted him aloft by the neck
then butchered him for a feast.

The toothless man laughed
at a man divided into parts.
Your soul appeared
you were upon the air
looking down at me.

Rosehips

Joseph encounters Rose on Popples Common

Her green cloak, the yellow leaves,
the red rosehips of the hedge.
Her cloak catches on thorns

is a phantom. I unhook it,
we begin to pick rosehips,
her fingers red with the syrup.

I tear my thumb and she licks it,
wraps a leaf about it,
soothing like a potion.

I ask will she be at church?
She will not kneel before a man
for she is married to Christ.

The sky becomes troubled,
rain falls softly, then faster,
holding her hair to her face.

Lodger

Alice Cockcroft on Sergeant Leach

The soldier billeted in my house
makes a play of manners as best as he can
but the campfire is where he belongs.

All his coin he has given me
for meat left on the bones
since he may not need it when the battle's done.

Blood swims in his eyes, slaughter he thinks upon,
the mother's sons he has cut open,
he sees as he chews the mutton.

His skin turned grey
the look of a wolf, the smell of a hound
coming off him, he sings to my son,

*We three Soldiers be
lately come from the Low Country,*
and his eyes in the darkness see.

Billet

Pike-man Sergeant Leach on his lodgings

I clap along to the woman's songs
but when I sing my soldiers' ditties
they hush me though her boy will say
Mother let him be.

Her son is restless, does not want
to walk the years ahead towards his father
rolling out the cloth thread by thread
only to shroud his manhood.

I have seen his father's eyes before
they are enemies of our cause
we awake to find they have deserted,
but the army could use his boy.

The weaver's life is small, his God a tailor,
he does not look up from his loom to the war
but speaks in corners with his wife,
I am a ghost upon a stool.

We sleep by the fire the four of us
the boy dreaming of a maid who loves a soldier,
his mother and father dreaming of a summer past,
a day of ale and cakes.

Cockcroft's Soldier

Joseph Cockcroft on Sergeant Leach

His age I cannot say and I will not ask
about the scars patched upon his arms,
all day he polishes his silver sword
like a dog licking at its paws.

He wears the roundhead hair of a boy
a smell from him I think is oil
he likes to sing to a tapping foot
songs he learned in Holland.

He makes light of driving a pike
into the breast of horses
some moments he stops his cloth
his thoughts inside past battles.

He talks each night inside his sleep
The first shall be last and the last the first
I wake to find his face above me
We must free the king from popish company

Spy

Squire Thornfield on Edmund Reeve

He is my man in Heptonstall
among the clothiers and whores
hiding his true self,
he says he fled from Halifax
plays the puritan to all.

His face is an autumn sky
his gaze wanders with the wind
temper with the moons
accusing then reprieving
the trust of fools does feed him.

Secrets he carries lightly
feathers in his cap
coded messages he leaves
for me I can read
but the man I cannot.

Sways as he walks even
unsure of his way
dark-eyed half-smiling
double dissembling
a heart forged from clay.

He lives in their camp
counting muskets and canon
gauging the merit of their soldiers
supping with their men
tupping with their women.

He tempts them all to treason
plots a path for the battle
that it might be won
holds enough hatred
to make two men out of one.

Wind of Doubt

The spy Edmund Reeve

The wind blows hard upon this hill,
there are blood red apples on the ground
and there are ghosts here too.

Yet you come to make more ghosts to be

yes of the roundheads who have climbed
to this perch, of the heretics, rats come
to the cuckoo's nest. The preacher Saltmarsh
pouring filth into the mouth of the girl Rose
who now drops his words about the shire
like leaves for others to turn to smoke.

You had him sent to the pillory for mere words.
Do you know what they did to him there?
They bored a hole in his tongue and cut off his ears.

They cut my father's innards out whilst he breathed

not for words, for plotting to blow parliament to hell

a defender of the faith as am I.
I am a spy and for that I must meet
and sleep with those I betray,
I must fix my Judas eyes against those
I select to die.

Are they the traitors or is it you?

They have stolen God,
like a piece of cloth
to walk around in shamble legged.

You would have welcomed the Armada,
they fight for England, you for Rome.

They fight for what they know.
The girl Rose will wield a cudgel
against charging cavalry

she will be stubble to their swords

trodden under foot like an acorn.

Days are dark, light and life short here and

I cannot think for this wind
which speaks to me.

Sinful

Joseph and Rose meet by the beck

The wind has left, the trees are still,
the water high and black. I sing to her,
Lavender's green, lavender's blue
You must love me for I love you.
She splashes my breeches,
her skirts about her knees,
her thoughts a secret.

She hums the melody but speaks of armies,
a martyr and a pilgrim called Edmund
come to join Bradshaw's men.
I speak of Christmas, of feasting and joy,
she says she must fast for the sins of mankind.

The sun wanes, we go to the woods
gather the leaves in a pile and lie.
A shadow skims between the trees,
she looks away, up to the burning sky
says it is a vixen come to feed.

Pilgrim

Rose on meeting Edmund Reeve

William brought unto me a man who escaped,
he rested his eyes on mine, said not a word.
Edmund his name, much beaten for his faith
in what waits beyond this inferior world,
he knows man as beast and man as Christ.

We walk together through the soldiers' camp
he offers to watch from the tower each night
the first to see the papists advance,
to toll the bell and the village awake.
He will lead the charge and I shall follow
with doe-eyed Joseph chasing my tail,
I must the girl and the boy bid farewell.
If I were a rosehip Joseph would chew me
Edmund, he will press his fingers through me.

Murder and Remorse

The spy Edmund, 30 October

The night after next I will sway my light
as dogs lay asleep beside embers.
Mackworth will come to take fathers from sons
make orphans and make widows. There will be
no fight, no quarter given, hovels alight
bodies rolled in to fires and trenches.

My action fears its consequence.
The girl Rose, that boy with more lice than sense
badgering me and the soldiers at camp
for some part to play in making his death.
I cannot stand and watch murder run rampant
I shall keep handsome Rose safe as best I may,
little ones I'll save as others hunt for prey
in houses where heresy is woven.

Fretful

John Cockcroft

Joseph has lost his wits over some lass
his mind a wasp
his face a kitten's in a quandary.

She is daily more about the village
with Joseph, with soldiers
and he dancing to her talk

about what she supposes God wants,
of the fight to come
as if it were a pace egg play.

Soldier Leach polishes his sword ever more.
I see him in prayer, muttering hard
in the middle of the day.

Joseph asks about cavalry and canon
I know he loiters about the camp
but I have not the work to give him.

Night March

*Sir Francis Mackworth leads his army to Heptonstall,
night of 1 November 1643*

We march from Halifax, the hour strikes four,
climb at the place they call Luddenden
then westward along the valley top before

sliding down to the swollen river flooding
all the fields east. We cross the bridge and wait,
the sky a sponge slumped on the hill above.

An otter seizes a duck breaking
it on the rocks. We must empty the nest
of roundheads, of heretics who defecate

in churches, who think blasphemy a blessing.
We will ascend a hundred feet times five
take the village from the blind, when our spy

in the tower signals, there will be no chimes,
we will slay them in their rat holes. There are
signs in the sky that mark the times:

God lights a fuse, the heavens ignite, firing
at the moon's blank face. Stars are born and dying.

Fight or Flee

Joseph Cockcroft, before dawn 1 November

The man in the watchtower is not a lookout
he is there to guide dogs up the hill
and they are coming, purple tongues
hanging, noses on the ground.

I saw him, this Edmund, rat-stooped
in the tower swing a lantern
his hand aflame, waving at the lights below.
The liar who scuttles beside Rose
along the lane, nods at soldiers in the camp
as if he were their comrade
has tricked them all but me
and must be seized then hanged, but after.

I can hold a sword, a pike
yet parliament will not arm me.
Father we must wake the street
go to the buttress throw rocks if we must,
but drive back the beasts that come at us.

Victory

*Pike-man Sergeant Leach at the Battle of Heptonstall,
1 November*

The boy Joseph has come from the tower
he runs about the streets calling,
a lamb without its herd
crying *alarm, alarm, they are here.*
His father calls him to his cottage,
the boy carries on bleating a battle cry.

Inside a mist upon the field
my men are at a cart
collecting pikes and axes,
I call them to me and we march
toward the clapping of hooves on stone.

Men, shoeless shaven-head boys
women even, scurry past us, through us,
jostle their way to the lip of the village.
Sprawling shadows of horses break under rocks
tumbling from the cliffs above,
one before me staggers to its end
I pike its rider, Joseph digs with his bodkin too,
we are about our business of making death.

The papists flee back to the river,
a rock tossed from on high,
from our own side
breaks the head of Joseph.
He lays on his back with the eyes of a trout.

Apology

Sir Francis Mackworth to the Earl of Newcastle, 3 November

Your Grace I must tell you
I tried to seize a hilltop village
called Heptonstall but have failed.

My man in the camp made his signal
my sodden men, the cavalry troop, we crept up the slope
when not a hundred feet from the flooded valley
rocks poured down as hail, tossed by phantoms.

The heads of horses bled, lay on the ground weeping
speaking of their pain, I pulled one rider
from under masonry and flesh
the beast's eyes were bright, questioning.
Horses turned back to the torrent; men followed
some swept under banks, we went with the river east.

The stone plungers have a savagery
the vengeance of centuries in their arms
and they have kept their crooked fort for now,
they will have swilled down and pissed out the victory
heresy running off the rocks.

Their minds think God gave them this day
he did so to stoke my rage
I read the heavens wrong
my man up there too, he led us into a lair.

I remain through you God's servant
and have some prisoners in Halifax I can attend to.
Vivat Carolus Rex.

God's Work

Alice Cockcroft

My last son run down the hill
never to run up again. Was it God
that dawn that took my careless one?

I was set against him growing,
counting his toes to him one minute
shoeing his feet to chase crows the next.

Lasses he didn't know, strange to him as fish
to a swallow, one though, the orphan Rose
caught his heart on the moor

tossed it up and down like a ball,
he saw pearls where there is coal
soft hands where there are claws.

She spoke to Joseph of God,
sent him running at swords and horses
under rocks pitched like bales of hay.

To know God you must have a child of God
then see them killed whilst still a child.
Grief spins into yarn that has no end.

Forsaken

The spy Edmund, taken prisoner by Parliament's army

Christ's words will not be heard or spoken
in an England that is so defiled
all its rituals all its magic taken.

The Church nailed to a cross and broken
by brutes who pray in fields among cattle
where Christ's words are not heard or spoken.

I live amid a faithless generation
weary now of this imperfect world
all its rituals and magic taken.

I am in chains forsaken by man awaiting
the gallows where I will be hurled away,
Christ's words not heard or spoken.

Though some may cheer at my execution
my martyrdom shall be a grey affair
all rituals and all magic taken.

England has become a seeded garden
fruitless and dreary, a viper's nest
where Christ's words are not heard or spoken
all its magic, all its flowers taken.

Did I Plant Anew?

*Colonel Robert Bradshaw lies mortally wounded upon his bed,
8 December 1643*

I went to war against my king for you,
my sword slew many men without mercy,
did I stain the earth, did I plant anew?

Are these wounds my death or my passage through?
Against the grey the birds fly in a vee.
I went to war against my king for you,

I fought faithful peasants and plough boys who
scratch the earth and pray on bended knees,
did I stain the earth, did I plant anew?

I am ashamed of what I had to do,
somewhere there are warmer days, greener trees.
I went to war against my king for you,

my soldiers sowed bloody death, it is true
there are more to grieve for than left to grieve,
did I stain the earth, did I plant anew?

Do men fight this war for me or for you?
The owl is out to hunt and I must leave.
I went to war against my king for you,
did I stain the earth, did I plant anew?

Ballad of the Battle of Heptonstall

The wheel turned upon the hill
Night turned to day
The river cried to the hills
Cavalry carried away

An army waited up above
Another gathered below
The village knew it would be blood
For the craggy place of old

Murder they kept from their homes
Murder best done below
Death was made upon the hillside
And where the river flows

Cavalry climbed the mossy stones
Before a cockerel cried
They rode at rocks and swords
They turned about or died

Horses died for their king
Menfolk died for colonels
People do such bloody things
With billhooks and with sickles

Some men killed for hatred
Some for God above
Some men killed for bread and ale
One boy died for love

Love and madness took his heart
Took a mother's son
Took him down to play his part
Life for a battle won

Cries of war swept the hills
The trees did shake and sigh
Death disturbed the very air
I heard a kestrel cry

The wheel turned upon the hill
Night turned to day
The river cried to the hills
Cavalry carried away

Visitor

Wool Master returns to Heptonstall, May 1644

I shall not climb this hill again
lead my labouring horse
its heavy head turning to look behind.

The cloth hall is closed
merchants fled like larks
the village an empty loft, a lonely maypole.

Pious men at arms spewed fever
into houses, into the school house,
spread sword play and wounds.

A horse comes snorting from the mist
dragging its reins in search of a rider
its hooves I cannot hear upon the ground.

It might have been an owl I heard last night
it might have been a weaver crying.
Not a soul speaks as I pass.

Aftermath

Cursed

Leveller Thomas Rainsborough at Westminster, January 2019

These houses are more adrift from England
than I was at Providence Island.
I walk the corridors of my dream
Members talk as masters of the kingdom
when they were sent here as its servants,
they crave the peoples' love yet think them imbeciles.

There sleeps the Lords among whom I search
for the descendants of those that killed me.
Did they come from here or were they sent by Oliver?
They have a plaque about me in Doncaster
upon the wall of the House of Fraser,
while Oliver has a statute outside Westminster.
King Jesus is still yet to come
All brethren of the free spirit gone.

Sealed Knot

It's a crush inside the block of pike-men
the cavalry circling, mocking my regiment of *foote,*
to them we are nothing but a brutish multitude
fit only for driving taxis and shielding musket men from riders.

I break from the ranks and bob between two horses,
slap another's arse sending the toff on top
into the hedge by the car park.

For that they used the phrase 'appalling behaviour'
in the regiment newsletter.
But where are men without battle, without a field to be won?
I am a true Leveller and a Lilburne man.

The horse is fine, the rider will recover in time
for Naseby. She says he forgives me.
A royalist forgiving a roundhead, imagine that.

Squaddie

He meets his regiment mates each week,
not at the Legion – not no more after what he said
to a former officer there.

They make plans over pints to occupy themselves,
short hikes and long-distance footpaths
days plotted from a to b.

He's worked out how to go from Sheffield to London by bus,
the routes, times, numbers all listed,
he briefs them on the expense the excursion will incur.

Under his shirt his back wears a relief map
of burns where a petrol bomb splashed up
from a street in Londonderry.

They sit at the back of the bus sipping cans,
talk about the coppers coming
for something that was done in Ireland,

what that Asian said to him on Poppy Day,
about six am on the parade ground
before he became someone else's job
and had to rely on people who don't show up on time.

Veteran in Recovery

In the dictionary between *shit* and *suicide*
is *sympathy*. That's where it belongs.

I learned to drink in the tank regiment.
Outlandish games in the mess each night,
no one dared stay on their bunk
with headphones on, a book, a pen and paper.

In the morning I learned not to run
behind a lad who'd had a skin-full.
The wind picks up the vomit
chucks it down the line.

The regiment colours are,
green for the grass we conquer,
brown for the mud we leave behind,
red for the blood we spill.

When we made the grade
the officers had us drink
a pint and a half of the same –
cranberry cocktail, liqueur and ale.

In eighteen years I barely fired a round.
I was drunk when I took my vows,
one over the eight when she slammed the door.

Now every day's a battle,
old regiment mates in the room each week,
we have each other's backs.

Soldier's Boy

My dad was in a jeep behind another jeep.
A boy walked up to the first one
and blew himself up.
My dad got out of the one behind
to help the wounded.

I know this because my sister told me.
She's old enough to get told stuff
or stay up late and listen.

Another time he was shot and nearly died
but he's all right now.
There's a medal in the house somewhere.

In September I start another new school,
I will miss my friends again.
Sometimes other kids aren't okay with you
when they hear your dad's a soldier.
Once this lad said he hoped my dad
has his head sawn off on youtube.

Chances Are

It chose me.
After two hundred exams,
psychometric tests,
interview selection,
Sandhurst,
an Arctic Warfare course,
failure as a linguist;
it took me into its breast.
Explosive Ordinance Disposal –
Every One's Divorced.

I'm not rock and roll,
some crazy arse.
Base jumping and motorbikes,
that's for foot soldiers.
I have blown Chance out like a match,
put away the playing cards,
swallowed my indefinite articles –
all other half measures.
My dreams are calculated.
a bomb strapped to a petrol tank
is a code to be broken.

Chance waits back there
at the perimeter
with my second Number Two.
Ahead, only the certain anarchy
of a breeze into my visor,
a mosquito towards my eye,
or the insurgent's crossed wires.

The enemy holds it breath
under the pale earth.
Its father is watching and filming;
this is getting silly.
I sweep the sleep away from its eyes,
bring it into the light,
put my hand over its mouth
until the last sigh.
When I come home
we will learn to love each other again.

The Hand That Crossed the Paper

after Dylan Thomas

The hand that crossed the ballot paper
Held a pencil attached to string
The mark I made has been erased
My open palm is called a fist

These five fingers felled the pound
I have no tears to flow
I am not afraid to leave behind
The masters I do not know

The hand that crossed the paper bears no shame
Nor did it cause some stranger's death
Nor can it touch the hand that holds dominion over
My daily bread, my place of birth

Five fields there were behind my house
Once beautiful, once for swallows
The woods for walks now built upon
Like promises made by lawyers

Arboriculture

In summer its leaves bank up in clouds
leaving his lawn like a goalmouth,
shadowing plans for alfresco dining.

Sunlight barely trickles through
so he will have it felled, sweep up
the ankle-deep drifts of leaves for the last time.

The patio builders arrive to measure up,
one testing the seams of an England shirt,
a country he no longer feels he knows.

He watches them from behind his kitchen window
hands on hips in a stance of reprimand,
overhears something said about *Polish pay rates*.

He takes his Retriever for a thoughtful walk
through the last of the woods before the by-pass,
before his son slams the door, drops his satchel in the hall.

He consoles himself with the memory that
it was him he had asked which way his father should vote.
He teaches him how to make cheese on toast.

He finishes a letter to *The Guardian*,
emails a friend who sits in the Lords
then rings the man with the chainsaw,
asks him if the oak could be made into a patio.

Fire-Bug

I wasn't bothered before.
Wasn't even sure which way I'd vote,
went back and forth.
Now people have stopped speaking to us,
they don't let on when we're walking the dog
they're so angry
you'd think we'd been keeping slaves in the shed.
Someone told me they'd been crying
like a child who's had his iphone taken
been given a Nokia instead.

I remember when there was a holiday with the school,
my parents couldn't afford to pay for it
but they wouldn't say.
They told the school I wouldn't be going
because I'd been bad, but I hadn't.
I was left behind with the kids from the bottom stream
whose parents didn't have the money either.
They took a holiday in the precinct,
I went to school and acted bad with Peter Whelan,
became his friend, sneaking past his snoring father
to get the matches from the kitchen,
lighting fires on the dump, waiting for fire engines.

Break-in at the Gallery of Justice

Little was taken from the small gallery
with not much in it.
A judge's broken gavel,
testimonies of survivors
we were sick of reading anyway,
a prosthetic limb carved out of shrapnel.

They left behind
a burglar's promise not to do it again.
Though the police didn't know and didn't show,
the break-in was probably an inside job.
The security guard was sacked
got drunk and killed his wife.

Hold That Thought

You are marched into the square
under a drum roll, a jury of Jackdaws
and upstairs windows.

Epaulettes torn from your shoulders,
your sword is improbably broken
across a journalist's knee.

Tied to the back of a funeral carriage
they drag you through television studios
scroll you across screens.

While you stand stooping in the stocks
screwed-up lines stuffed in your mouth,
you realise the ground you stand upon

was born and raised upon,
was only a scaffold after all.
A policeman will call

to discuss your thinking
because you were the first to stop clapping
the last to speak out of turn

out of time, sync, order, step,
and out loud you fool
what were you thinking?

Whatever it was or will be, don't.
Splay your fingers away
from the biro, the keyboard,

bunch them up in a pocket
then hold the thought,
squeeze it until it lives no more.

The Village

It is eleven years since we came here,
we are weathering in.

The winter village is itself.
Moss on stone on mud it knows.
We sink in inch by inch
under skies stolen from Turner.

In summer it feels defeated
by visitors stooping over handle bars,
off-roading into the car park
to look for a coiner's or a poet's grave.

I look to the abandoned hawthorn humps
fancying a fox is sleeping there
but know any one of a hundred dogs
would put paid to that.

In the churchyard another tree is cut down
that a roundhead would have pissed against.

It is trees and stone and cars
jostling for space, the bones
of ruins forced to the surface
by the crowded world below.

On the tower of the old church
where they watched for the royalist army
barn owls nest year upon year,
as rare in England now as understatement.

On June nights we wait for its flight,
the slow strokes beating out a silence,
the glow from its wings remaining,
until we're wakened by the scream.

We plant seeds at the foot of lampposts,
there is a prayer hole in Foster Wood.

Gone

after Larkin

In my time I've seen so many go –
local woods and unfarmed grasslands
harmless fields left aside,
the rabbit wastes architects are apt to conquer,
they've all gone - more or less.

Towns merge like mercury. It's as if
the dragonfly retreats were never there.
National parks remain – ornaments in a house clearance
but really the countryside we have is on a lead,
beyond the passenger seat, behind the television.

It was never meant to begin with
but now I think it is. The old trees
are an afterlife from a country
we cannot bear to grieve for,
it is wrong now to go against concrete and tyres.

We were lucky my boys and me.
We had a Camelot where gypsies parked up
to run their horses and chain their dogs,
we lit fires and threw our knives
from a dozen paces. How quickly
we became bricked over.

Heptonstall Garden in June

The hillside knows it doesn't have long
in the sun of only weeks, the restless summers,
nervous as a chaffinch.

I wait for the Laburnum to show
to catch up with the Rowan and the Birch
watch the Iris swords grow

and hold the symmetries of a fern
that begin in my palm and end in shadow.
Everything up here is said at once.

We too were late to come to each other.
Where was I before when we were on the valley floor
during the slow summers?

We work at the edge of evening
through a frenzy of midges,
lie down with the blind half-closed,
a pheasant crows, thrums its wings.

Low Pressure

Wind keeps the sparrows from the feeder, plays
the roof tiles, the willow. A stream has risen
in the field. In the intervals of daylight
I watch it broaden, deepen. The lane wants
to be a river, water has filled up
ditches, fouled up sockets, crawled under doors.
The news piped through from Paris is of slaughter;

at least the storm has a name. I open the door
to a hedgehog curled up in a tyre track,
lift it to a gap in the graveyard wall.
We pack for the long haul to Sydney's
bright smiles that will blind me like a mole
torn into sunlight out of his dark home,
flooded ground still living in my bones.

Pub Landlord West Yorkshire

He always looked so fed up.
Like his muted dog,
sullen eyes, bony arse turned at solitary drinkers.

His beer was rotten.
Each pump offering a hangover
before you could empty your glass,
leave it foaming on the bar.

He didn't clean his lines.
Barrels hung around longer than customers
who only spoilt the atmosphere.
Many left without words,
their endurance shorter than a barmaid's.

A few of us remained,
we came to learn the meaning of loyalty,
decorum, the collywobbles.
Women rarely came in to kill the conversation.

Walkers, tourists, people who wanted food,
Does it bloody say food outside?
Stupid buggers who wanted a room.
After hours non-smokers were told to go outside.

He said he owned it and I believed him.
Offered to sell me the furniture
from behind his antique handkerchief.
I heard he'd done time for a friend, as a favour.

Farmers came in on Fridays for pie and peas,
the rest of the week I sat on my seat
back against the wall,
under the rules and the list of the barred,
sharing a bag of soft peanuts
with the coalman and a psychotherapist.

I floated through the bottom of days
like the white flakes I drank
in the middle of my glass,
until the brewery turfed him out
to a caravan where his dog died
and I gave up my seat,
for a pub like any other.

Dogs Own Country

I pass two women on the street
Jack Russell yelping at their heels
'He's finding his teenage years difficult.'
'Well, don't they all'
I didn't know she had a son.
'The vet said he needs more exercise.'
Well, not a homo sapien one.

Another one arrives every week
sniffing my crotch it greets me
leaves its gifts at the feet of lampposts,
sweet thing making its mark on pub furniture.
Another hound on a man's lap
licks his lover's lips for a Dorito
as a rescued pit bull claims the next table.

In my dream, the lion-sized one
I said sorry to for tripping over,
bans me from the establishment.
I can take them or leave them but here
they love them and need them, and
clutching little black bags in their hands
they tell me their star-signs.

St Thomas the Apostle Church, Heptonstall

Gothic beacon rubbing up against
the ruins of St Thomas a' Becket;
doubt and faith sharing the same graveyard.

Its vastness is unexpected.
Hollowed of pews, of its rood screen
and any woodwork bar the benches,
it is a chamber furnished by light,
echoes that split the chilled air.
Only a fool would produce a play in there.

Twenty or so scatter themselves around
then kneel in the communion queue,
but on evenings there are full houses
for quizzes and concerts, country dancing and theatre.

We rehearsed all winter,
turning up the heating bill
and I arriving before the actors,
earlier and earlier each night.

There is no need
to pace the aisle anymore
but still I go back, to be alone
in the company of absence.

Keighley Railway Museum

The dregs of a day.
Tight-fisted Pennine sky.
Light falls exhausted on the four of us,
the only customers come
to the platform's edge, the year's end
red nosed and gift wrapped.

We begin walking the carriages
fingering the headrests,
sit amidst the balmy sound effects
hands stroking the arm rests,
cat faces rubbed against the fabric,
eyes walking all over the wood grain,
the leg room, the creamy poster folk.

I close my eyes and wait
for a man in a waistcoat,
a cap he touches as he tells us
we will shortly arrive
at some grassy summer's afternoon
through a tunnel of birds, bees and elm trees
for blancmange, Brylcreem and leaf tea,
where if we look hard, we shall see
a boy in spectacles and shorts
bat a ball to a boundary.

You have brought home from Sydney
a man who dozes towards
our snug little country
we're sure was once there.
We leave through the gift shop,
to be carted away in the grey
from somewhere further,
somewhere approaching home.

The Day-Trip

Nine years old, my father takes me
up the line then underground
to see the waxworks, the scarlet throne,
the purple crown, the executioner's block
with cuts across its centre,
Henry's painted lances, the satin pillows
held down on the princes' faces.
I lean out like the condemned,
slip my fingers into the river.

Lying under a canopy of arches
sleeping in slow lines, a hundred men.
We walk among them, through them, to the tube.
I stumble into one, the bundle stands
wearing newspaper, wearing plastic,
eyes inches deep, numb as history
his head a hedge for a naturalist.
He does not speak, he waits
lets me look, then turns into darkness.

Plagued

Rats are crawling under the skin of our house
between the brickwork and the plaster
the ceiling and the loft,
hesitating between one sound and another

moving quickly, close to me,
I shout and they pause, close my eyes
they lick their whiskers, claws
clenched on blue cables.

The rat-man comes, puts down poison
says they are suspicious creatures
calls them neophobic, and
we wonder if they have met him before.

We itch, are unclean, are barely-slept
refugees traipsing about with pillows,
they run alongside us behind walls.
Come morning the rat-man scratches at our door.

Incurable

I must have swallowed it.
Like the sweet I took from my mother's pocket
lipstick red it smiled when I twisted off the wrapper,
I coughed so hard she dropped her ashtray
held me by my ankles and shook it out of me.

I must have touched something
like the time I helped my father concrete a path.
I watched its flawless surface harden by the minute,
carving my name with a wooden spoon
he burned my ear with the back of his hand.

I should have done what I was told
I went to railway arches instead of school.
Leaning on a shadow, burning a hole in the afternoon
a policeman brought me home.

I should stay in here with my symptoms
but I'm leaving for the high-street
to rub shoulders with window shoppers,
there is something that I need.

Aftermath

There was a war for a while.
Soldiers in the precinct,
one camouflaged for the desert outside JD Sports.
My history student tearful,
she knew someone who was there
had thought about going herself.
I saw photos on social media that were taken down.
A state of emergency, threat level bursting the barometer,
celebrities rushing to forgive in the crush to be calm
speaking well of the dead before the dead had finished dying,
seven days of hellish scenarios
then the soldiers went away and there was peace.

Peace with anything talked about except...
no not that again, not this evening, please
the peace of vanishing sleep
eight years old
of looking around you but not looking too long
what are they talking about, that one with the bag?
The frightened peace before a knock at the door,
the phone call number withheld, *why won't she pick up?*
The peace that finds you watching war films,
the ones where we win in the end,
an end?
The kind of peace where you think a lot more about death,
about killing.

Last Day of the Shrine

The cleaner stands behind me
holding his broom, his unfurled binbag,
like a herald waiting on my answer.

Most mornings people stop
stand beside me, sip their coffee and go.
It's not time yet, I tell him.

He asks if I want a keepsake
the teddy bear or a tee shirt
the flag on which the names are listed?

Rubbish over railings isn't why I'm here,
the bomb went off across the road
but they wouldn't let me stand there.

I glimpse her now and then
holding her mother's hand turning into school,
her light blue cardigan.

A shrine is where people pretend
they haven't forgotten,
the nails in her chest, the child's coffin.

I have been swept around this past year
I must go into town with the crowd
look for someone there.

Back and Forth

There are those that would have weavers make laws,
the word of God spoken on corners.
Would have all men reading, women speaking in church,
not knowing the greater part of the people
is not the better part.

Not everyone should be allowed to vote.
Some have minds that are willow to the wind
and others will be dead soon anyway.
Those not fit to climb the stairs
imagine they know how we should be governed,
tipping their failures into a ballot box.

>He that lives in a ditch has a better view
>of the fields than a man on a throne.
>The man behind a plough knows the price
>of corn better than a merchant.
>We who stand in the queue for a contract
>that adds up to nothing have lived before.

Acknowledgements

Several of these poems have previously appeared in *Poetry Salzburg Review, London Grip, The High Window* and *Close to Home* (Prole Books). I would like to thank poets Sarah Corbett and Andy Croft for their editorial advice on a number of the poems.